How to use Superhero Phonic Readers:

⭐ These stories are perfect for children who have learnt their letters and sounds in school. Start at level one and gradually progress through the series. Each story is a little bit longer than the last and uses more grown-up vocabulary.

⭐ Children will be able to read **Superhero Phonic Readers** for themselves. Let your child read to you, and share the excitement!

⭐ If your child finds a word difficult, help him or her to work out the sounds in the word.

⭐ Early readers can be concentrating so hard on the words that they sometimes don't fully grasp the overall meaning of what they read. The puzzle questions on pages 28 and 29 will help with this. Have fun talking about them together.

⭐ The Ladybird website **www.ladybird.com** features a wealth of information about phonics and reading.

⭐ Enjoy reading together!

Geraldine Taylor - Ladybird Educational Consultant

Educational Consultant: Geraldine Taylor
Phonics Consultant: Marj Newbury

A catalogue record for this book is available from the British Library

Published by Ladybird Books Ltd
80 Strand, London, WC2R 0RL
A Penguin Company

2 4 6 8 10 9 7 5 3 1
© LADYBIRD BOOKS LTD MMIX
LADYBIRD and the device of a Ladybird are trademarks of Ladybird Books Ltd

ISBN: 978-1-40930-156-1

Printed in Italy

Superhero
Phonic Readers

Zain Zoom

written by Mandy Ross
illustrated by Ingela Peterson

This is Zain Zoom as a baby.
He is very speedy.

This is Zain Zoom as a boy.
He is very, very speedy!

Zain Zoom was training to be
a superhero.

"I need a superhero skill," said Zain. "I must be super speedy."

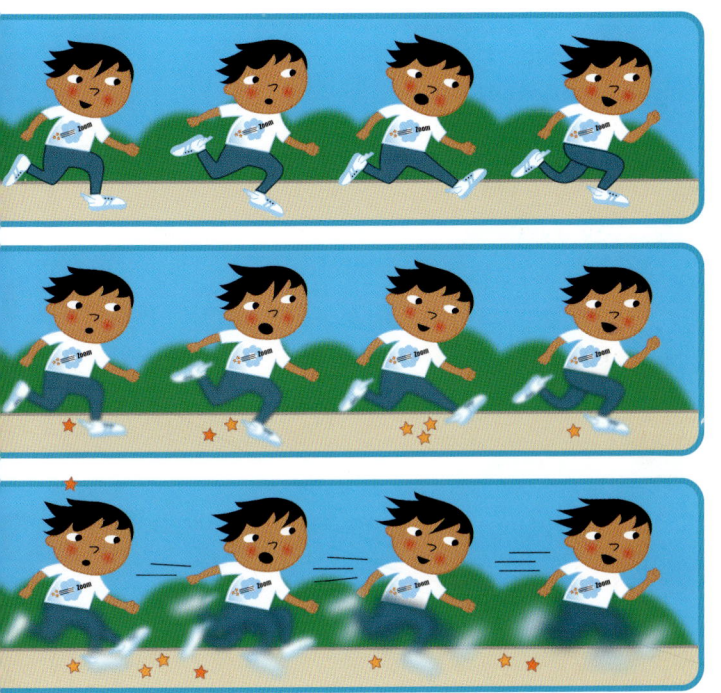

Zain runs and runs. He runs
up hills. He runs down hills.
He runs in zigzags.

He runs in the sun.

He runs in the rain.

Soon, Zain was faster than a car, or a train, or a plane!

Now, Zain is ready to be
a speedy superhero.

"Miss Viper has got my dog!"
says Mr Poodle.

Mr Poodle runs after Miss Viper, but he is too slow to catch up with her.

Miss Viper was very fast, but she was not super speedy like Zain.

Zain runs after her.

Miss Viper says,
"I need to go faster."
She jumps into a car.

Zain Zoom runs after the car.

Do not do this at home, readers.

Miss Viper says,
"I need to go faster."
She jumps from the car
onto a train.

Zain Zoom runs after the train.
Do NOT do this at home, readers.

Miss Viper says,
"I need to go faster."
She jumps into a plane.

Zain Zoom runs after the plane.
NEVER do this at home, readers.

Zain Zoom catches up with the plane and turns the motor off. You CANNOT do this at home, readers.

Zain grabs Miss Viper and Pooch.
What a superhero!

Pooch is happy to see Mr Poodle.

Mr Poodle is happy to see Pooch.

PC Plod is happy to see Miss Viper.

Miss Viper is not happy to see
PC Plod.

And everybody is happy to see
Zain Zoom.

"Happy to help," says Zain Zoom,
the super speedy superhero.

Superhero Secret Puzzles

⭐ What is Zain's super skill?

⭐ Who does Pooch belong to?

⭐ Who stole Pooch?

⭐ How did Zain Zoom stop the plane?

⭐ Are you super speedy?

Look at these pictures from the story
and say the order they should go in.

A

B

C

D

Answer on page 30.

Tricky Words Memory Quiz

Can you remember these
words from the story?

See if you can read them super-fast.

he	I	my	her	into
to	the	Mr	she	what
be	do	go	you	

What else can you remember?
Can you put the book down
and say what happens in the story?